D0031740

A WORD ABOUT THIS BOOK

In 1953 my father, Mervyn Peake, moved with his family — Sebastian, Clare, and myself — to a large Victorian house in Surrey. My father had lived there before with his parents while he attended the Royal Academy Schools. And it was there that the idea for FIGURES OF SPEECH germinated. With my mother, Maeve Gilmore, he drew up a list of popular sayings and chose examples that would lend themselves most readily to illustration. It was a time when much of his work was of a serious nature, and the light-hearted spirit of this book must have been a welcome relief — in comparison, as easy as falling off a log! And now, in this new edition, the guessing game my father devised can be enjoyed all over again.

FABIAN PEAKE

LONDON, DECEMBER 2002

Mervyn Peake

FIGURES OF SPEECH

CANDLEWICK PRESS
CAMBRIDGE, MASSACHUSETTS

❖ ❖ ❖ ❖ ❖ ❖ ❖   PUBLISHER'S NOTE   ❖ ❖ ❖ ❖ ❖ ❖ ❖
FIGURES OF SPEECH was first published in 1954. For this
new edition we have returned to Mervyn Peake's original
black ink drawings and reoriginated them with the
addition of color tints. The original printed text has
been reset in Golden Cockerel. We are grateful to Fabian
Peake and the Estate of Mervyn Peake for their support
and encouragement during the making of this edition.

❖

FIRST U.S. EDITION 2003. LIBRARY OF CONGRESS
CATALOGING-IN-PUBLICATION DATA IS AVAILABLE. LIBRARY OF CONGRESS CATALOG CARD
NUMBER 2002041757. ISBN 0-7636-2176-5. 10 9 8 7 6 5 4 3 2 1 PRINTED IN CHINA. THIS
BOOK WAS TYPESET IN GOLDEN COCKEREL. THE ILLUSTRATIONS WERE DONE IN INK.
CANDLEWICK PRESS, 2067 MASSACHUSETTS AVENUE, CAMBRIDGE, MASSACHUSETTS 02140
❖ ❖ ❖ ❖ ❖ ❖ ❖   VISIT US AT WWW.CANDLEWICK.COM   ❖ ❖ ❖ ❖ ❖ ❖ ❖

CONTENTS

We give no table of contents here, for to do so would spoil your pleasure. Each drawing represents a particular Figure of Speech. If you cannot identify it, you will find a key at the end of the book.

1

2

3

5

7

8

10

11

13

14

15

16

17

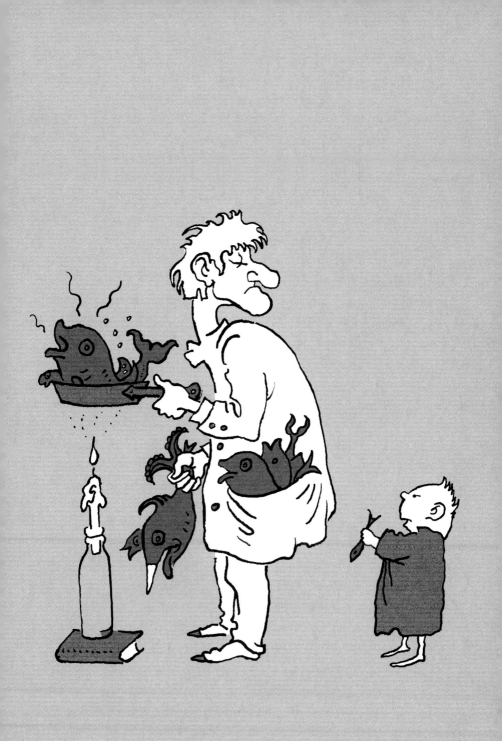

18

19

20

21

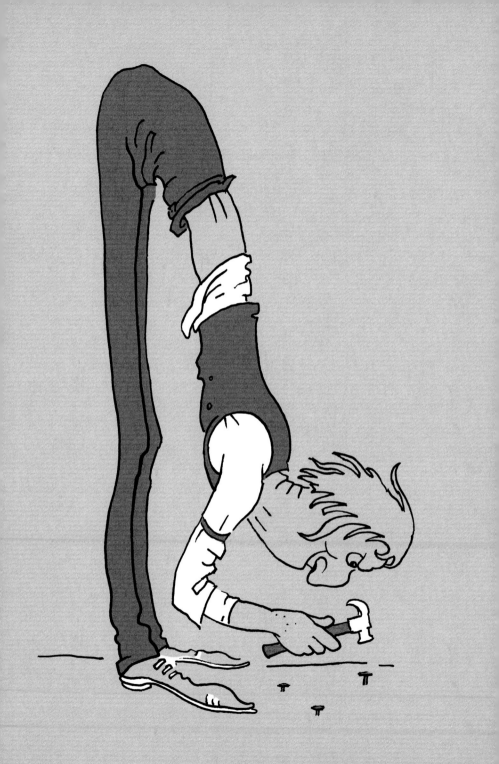

22

23

24

25

29

1. *You scratch my back,*
   I'll scratch yours.

2. *Love me, love my dog!*

3. *Burning their bridges*

4. *Grin and bear it.*

5. *Horseplay*

6. *Light-fingered*

7. *Holding up his end*

8. *A bird in the hand*
   is worth two in the bush.

9. *His right-hand man*

10. *Keeping his chin up*

11. *Led by the nose*

12. *Sitting pretty*

13. *Coming up to scratch*

14. *Getting his back up*

15. *Bringing him down to earth*

16. *To cut a long story short*

17. *I have other fish to fry.*

18. *It suits them down*
    to the ground.

19. *Severing relations*

20. *Put that in your pipe*
    and smoke it.

21. *Getting down*
    to brass tacks

22. *It came to a head.*

23. *Cooling his heels*

24. *Toeing the line*

25. *Splitting hairs*

26. *Paddle your own canoe!*

27. *Getting his sea legs*

28. *Cold comfort*

29. *I could just kick myself.*